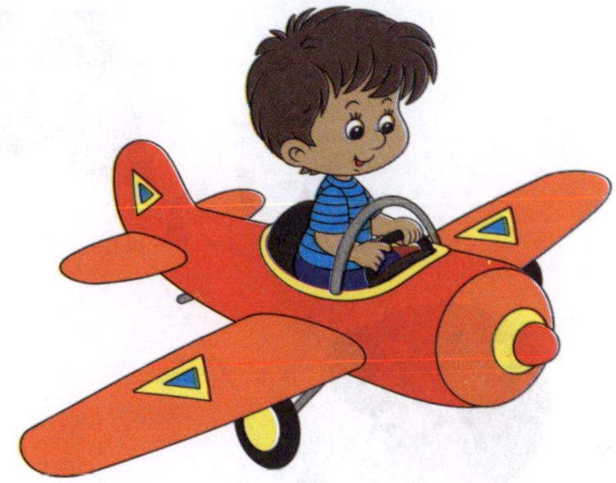

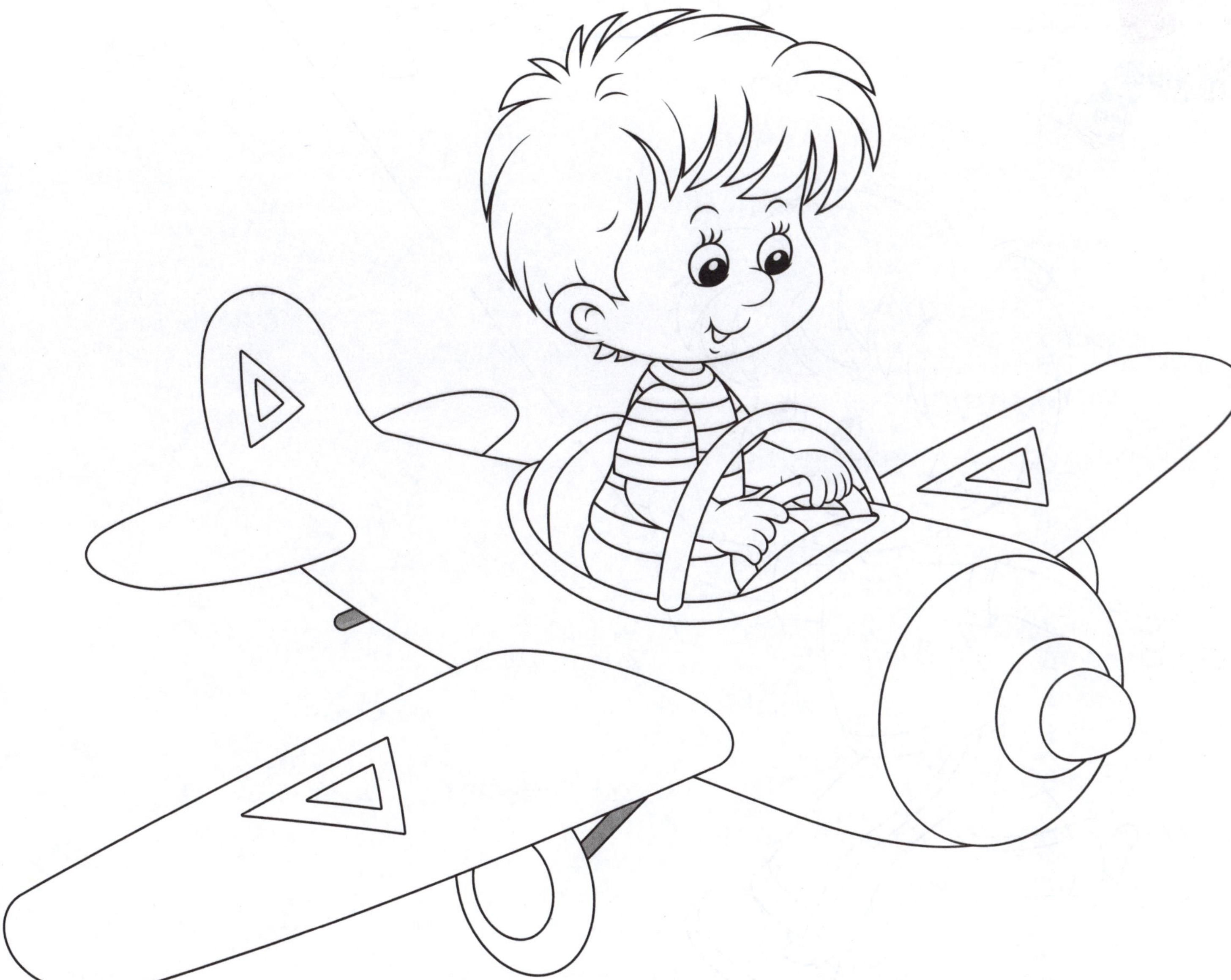

toy plane

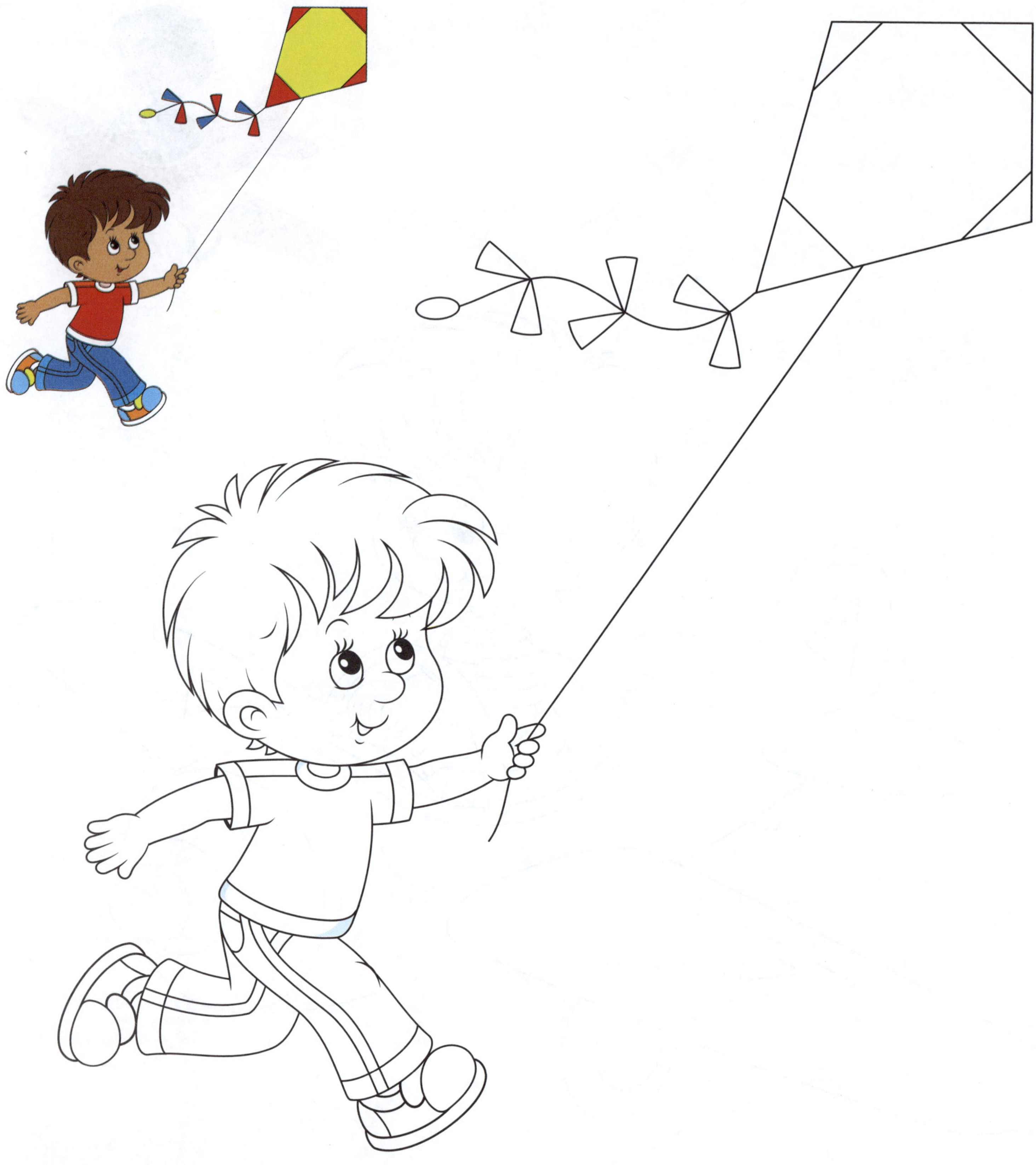

kite flying

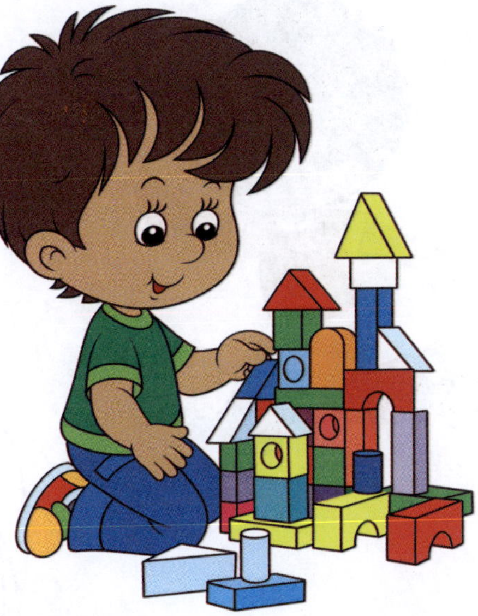

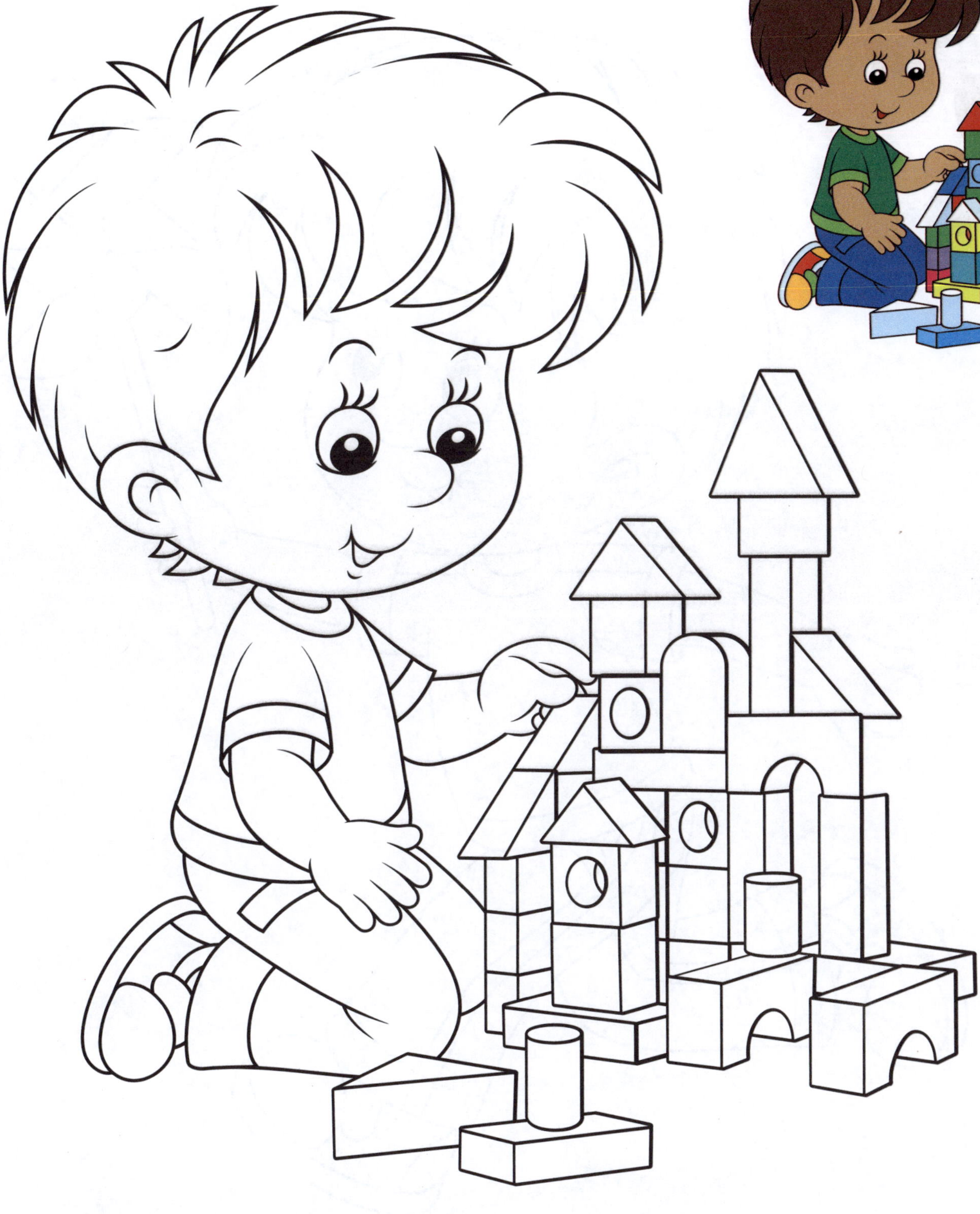

building blocks

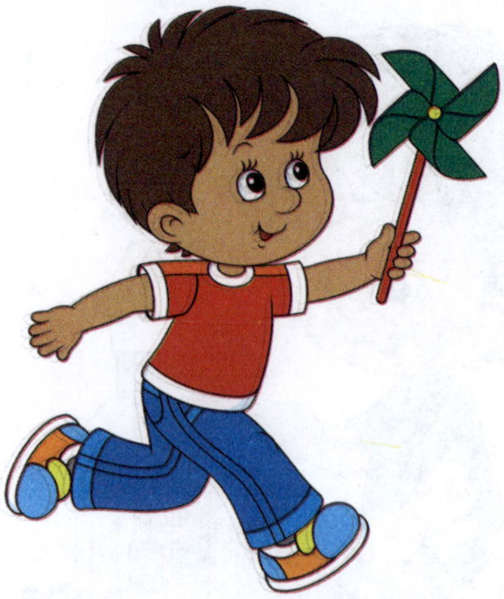

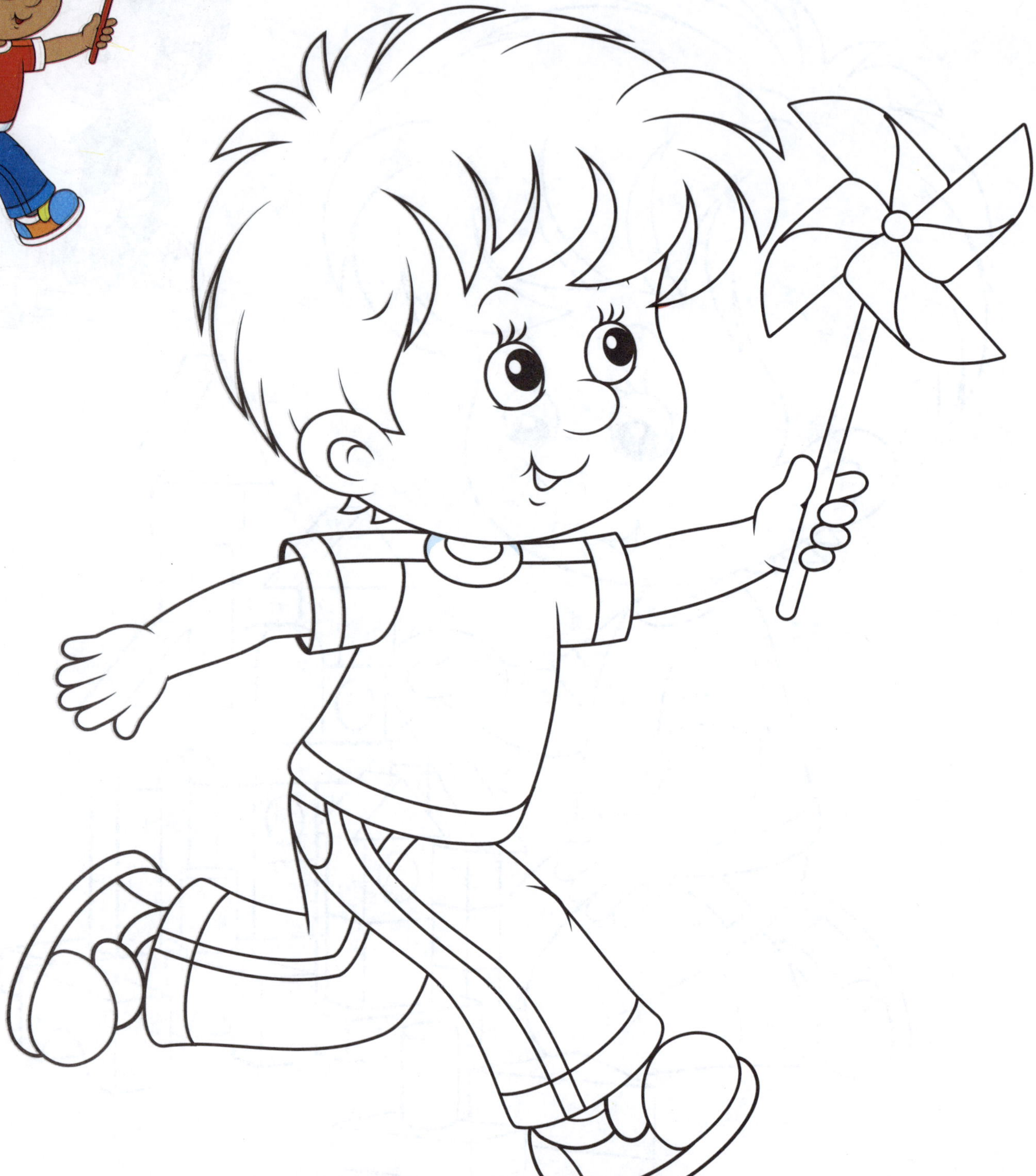

whirligig

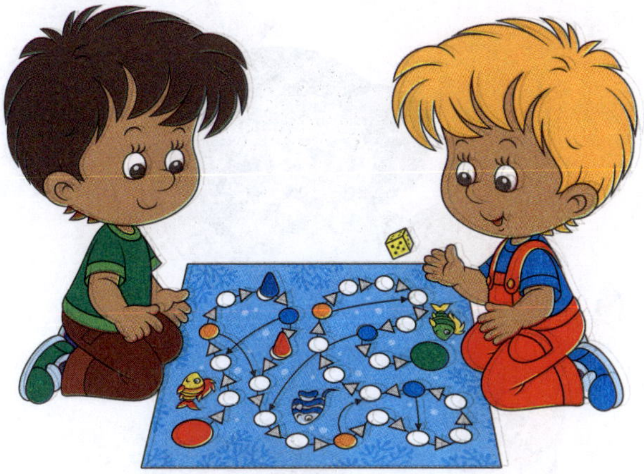

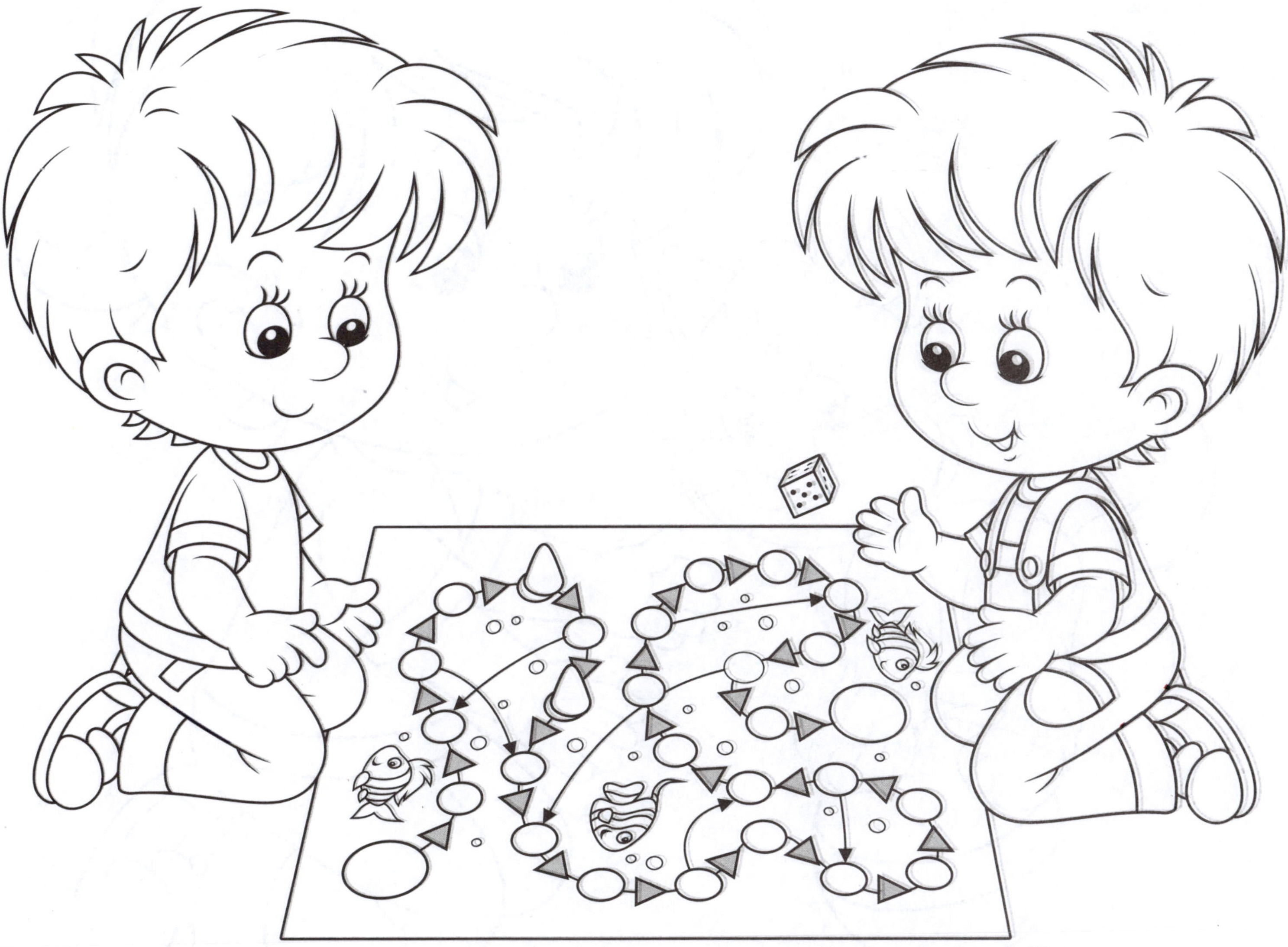

board game

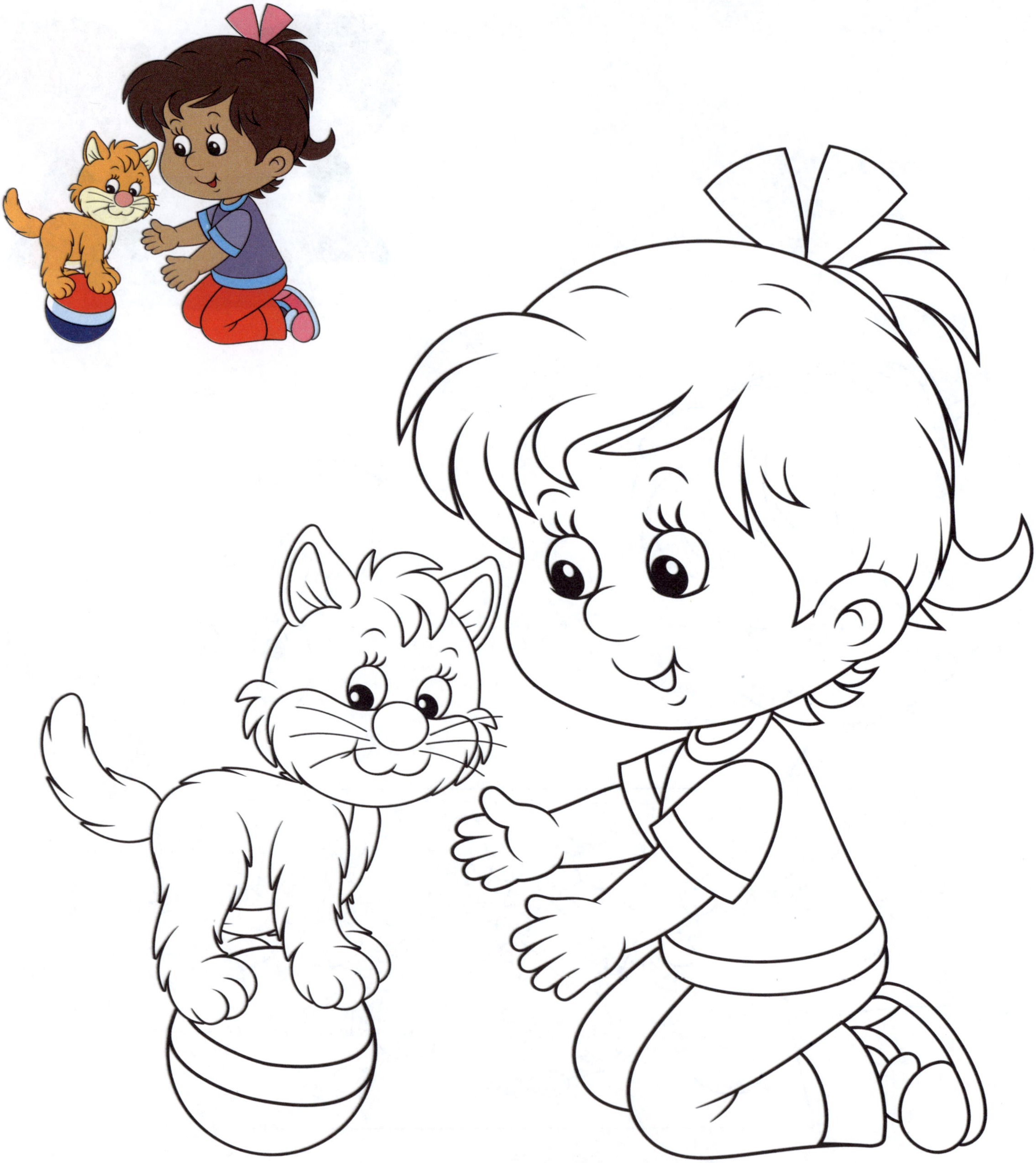

pet time

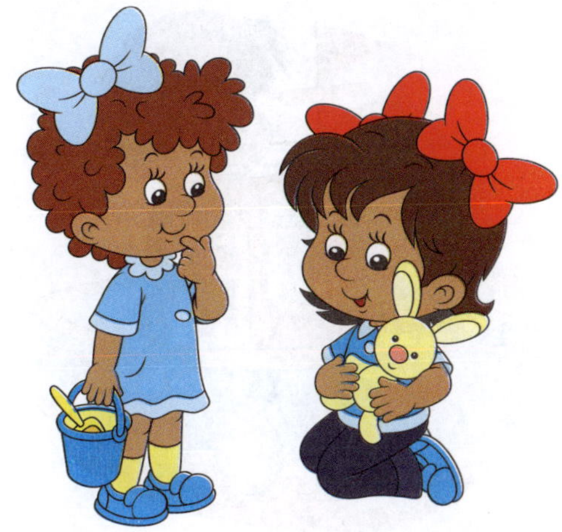

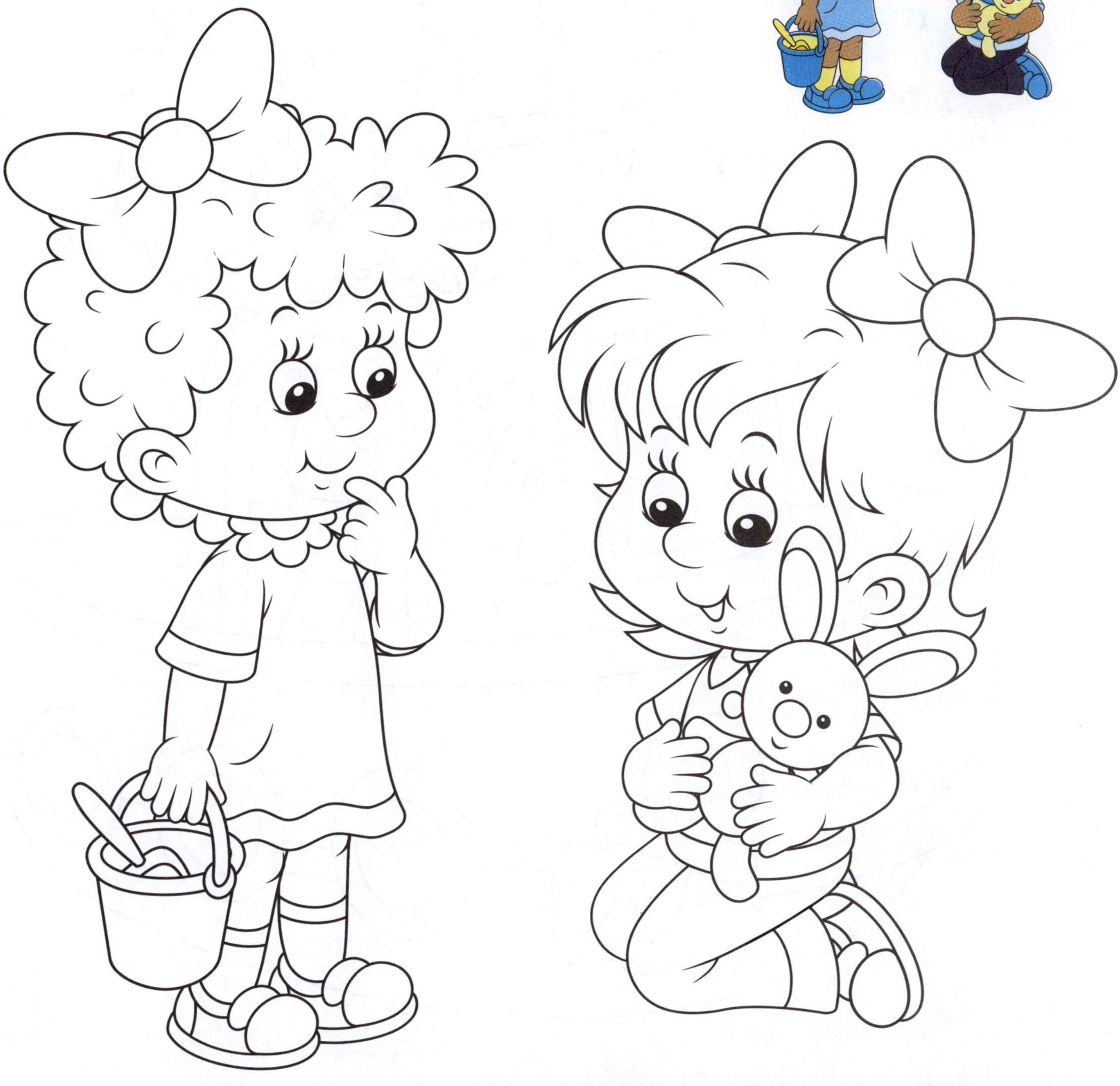

fun with friend

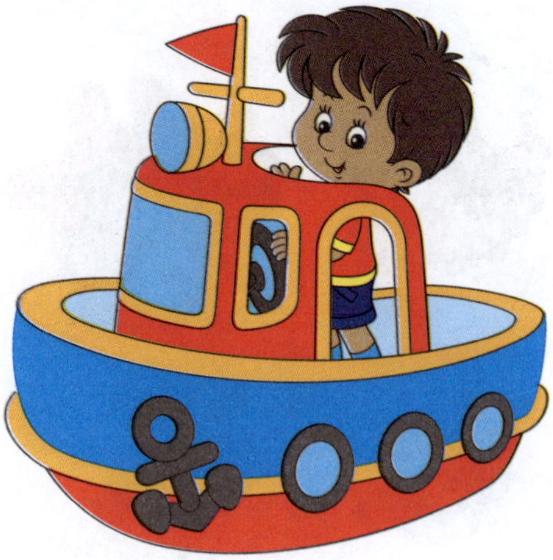

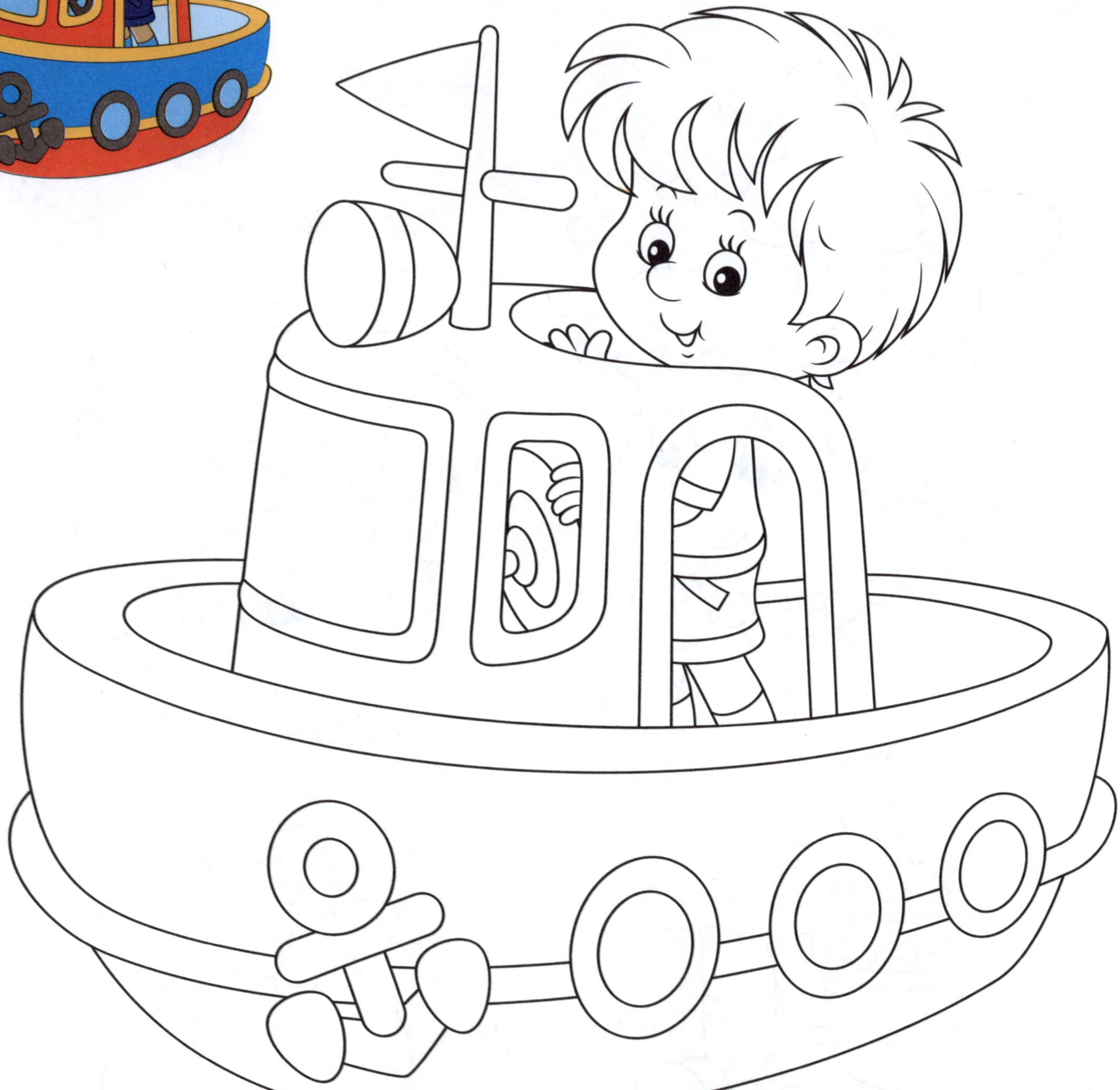

toy ship

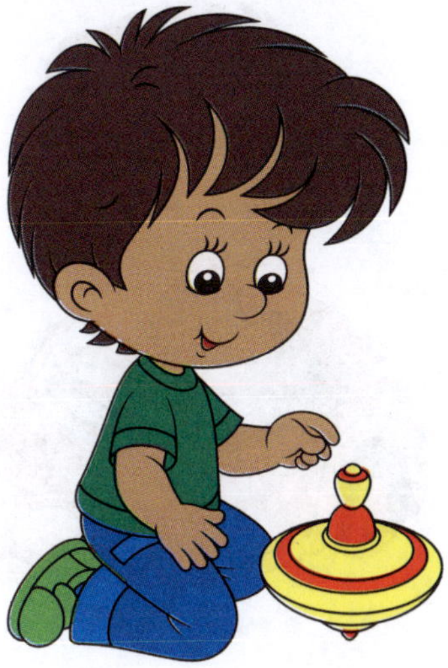

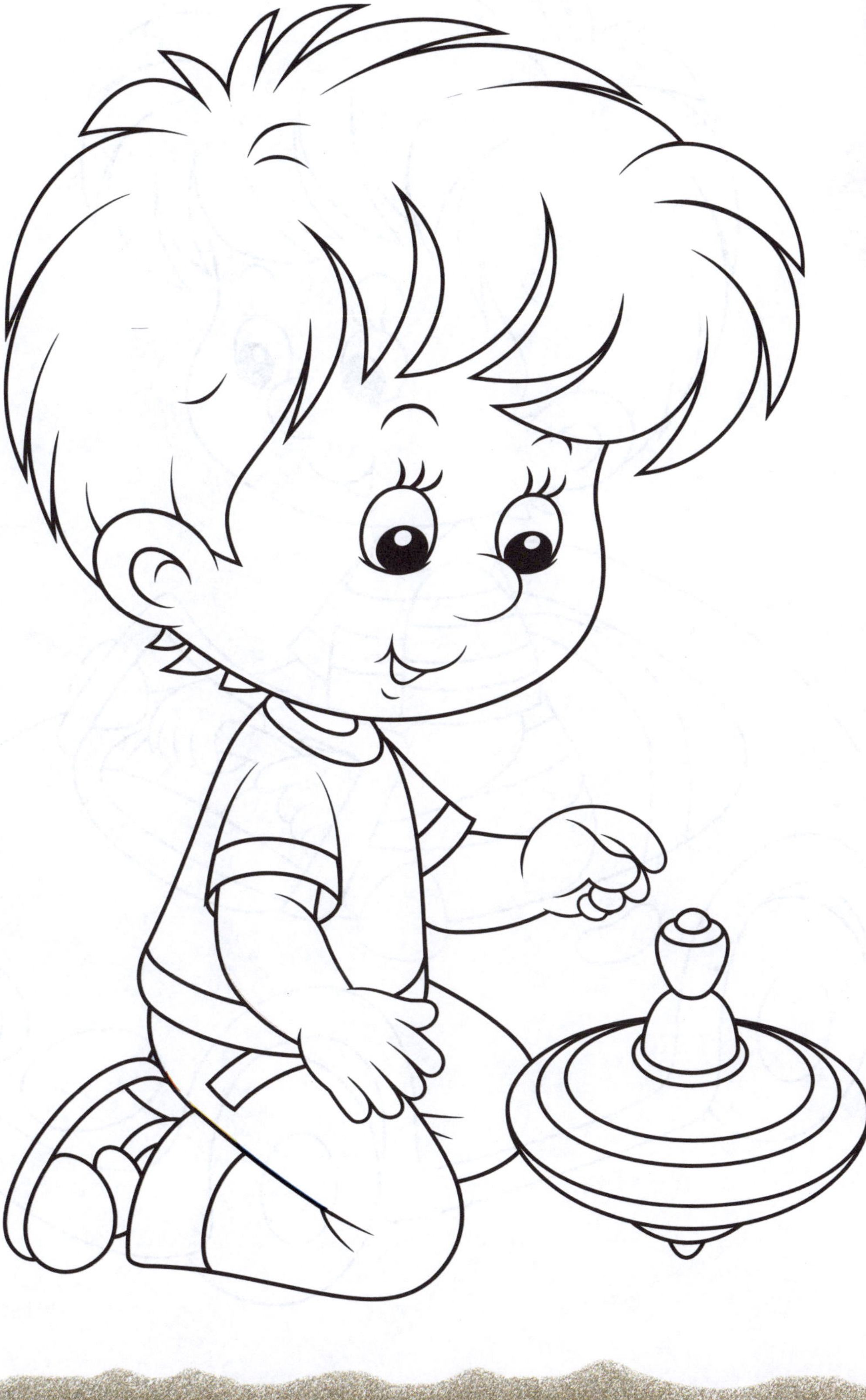

spinning top

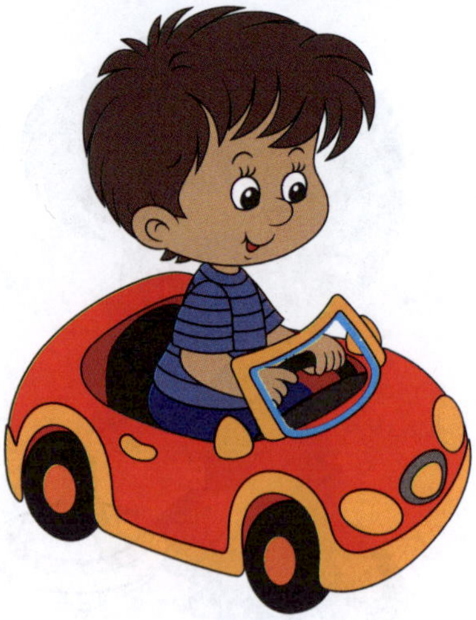

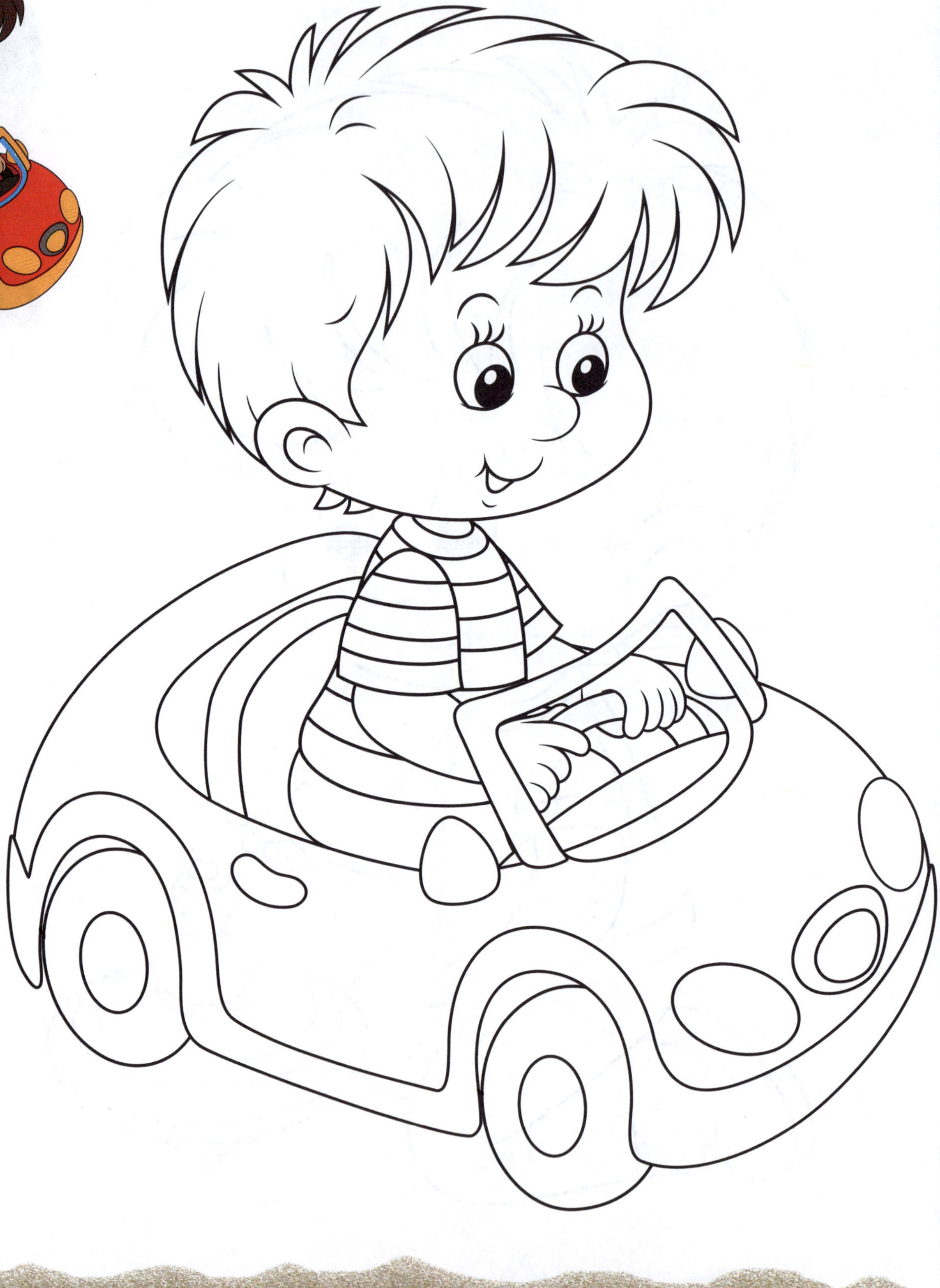

toy car

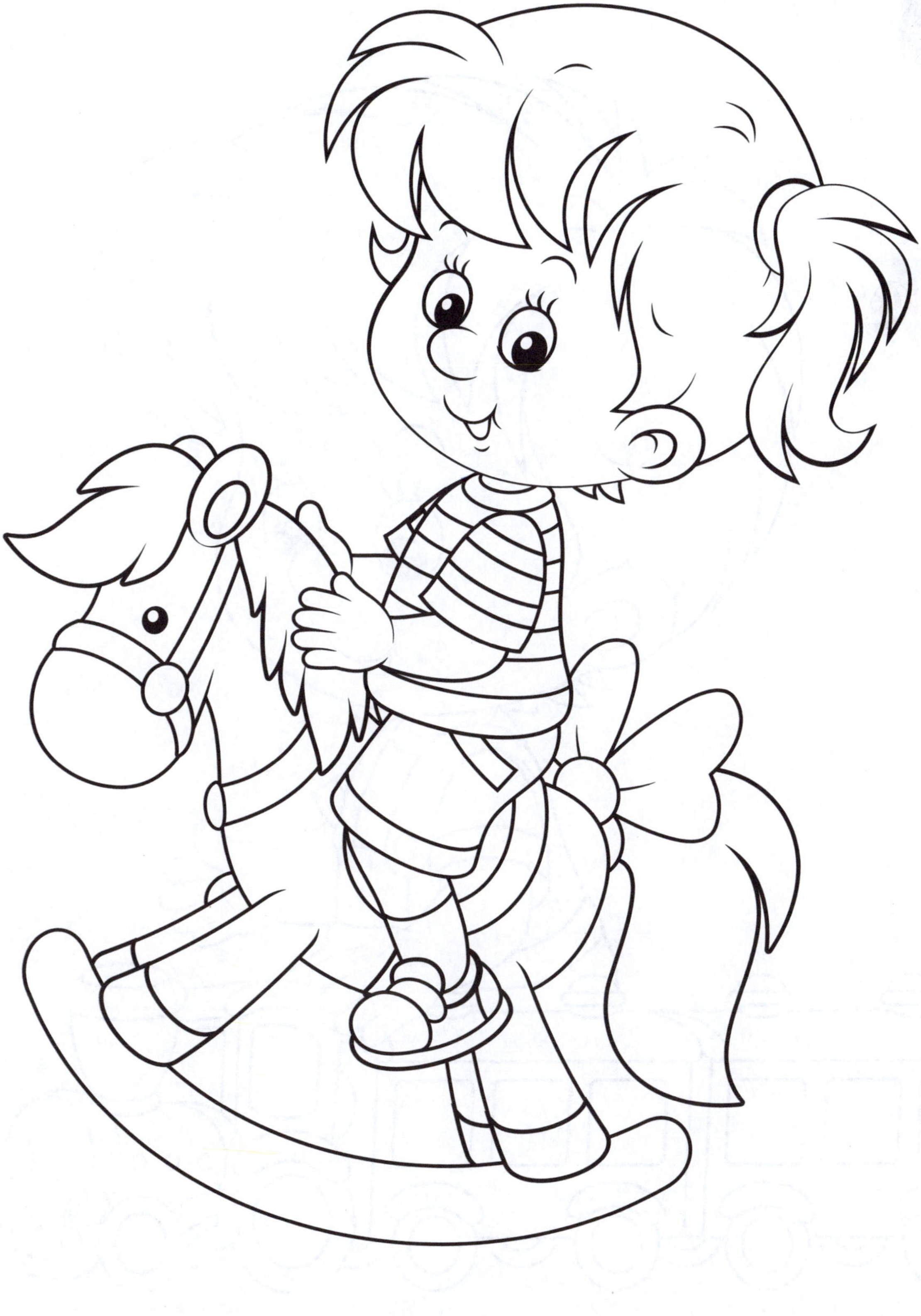

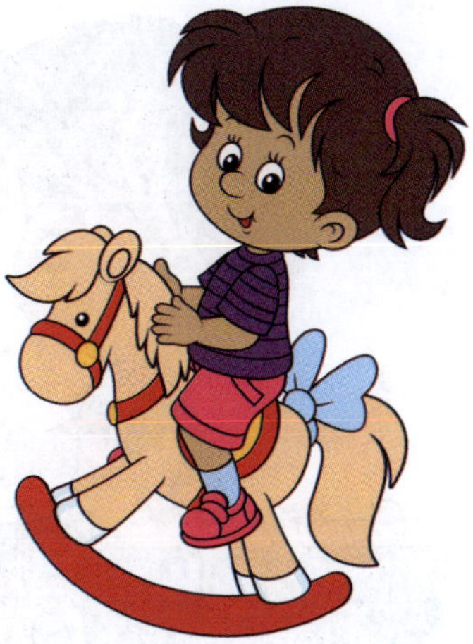

rocking horse

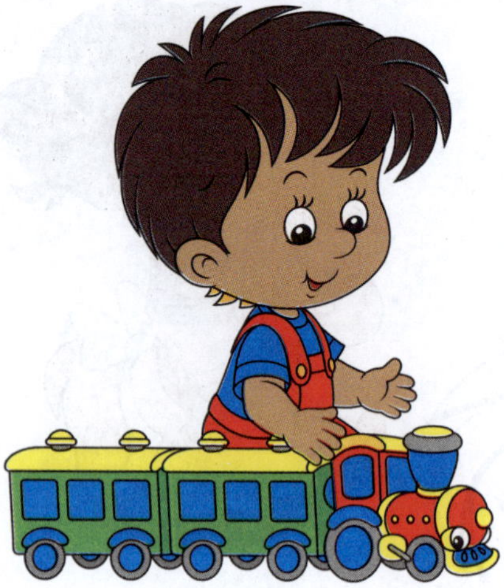

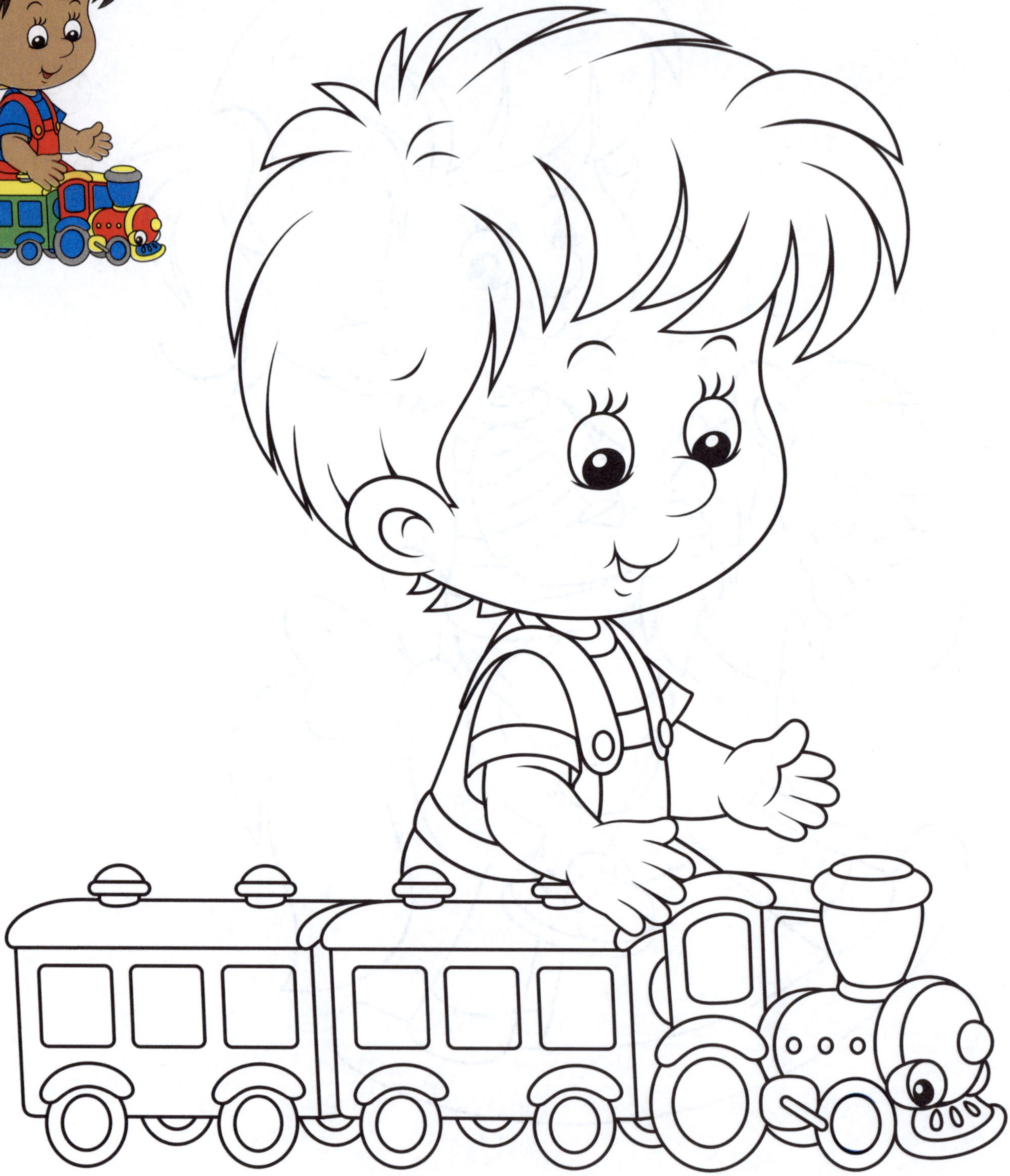

toy train

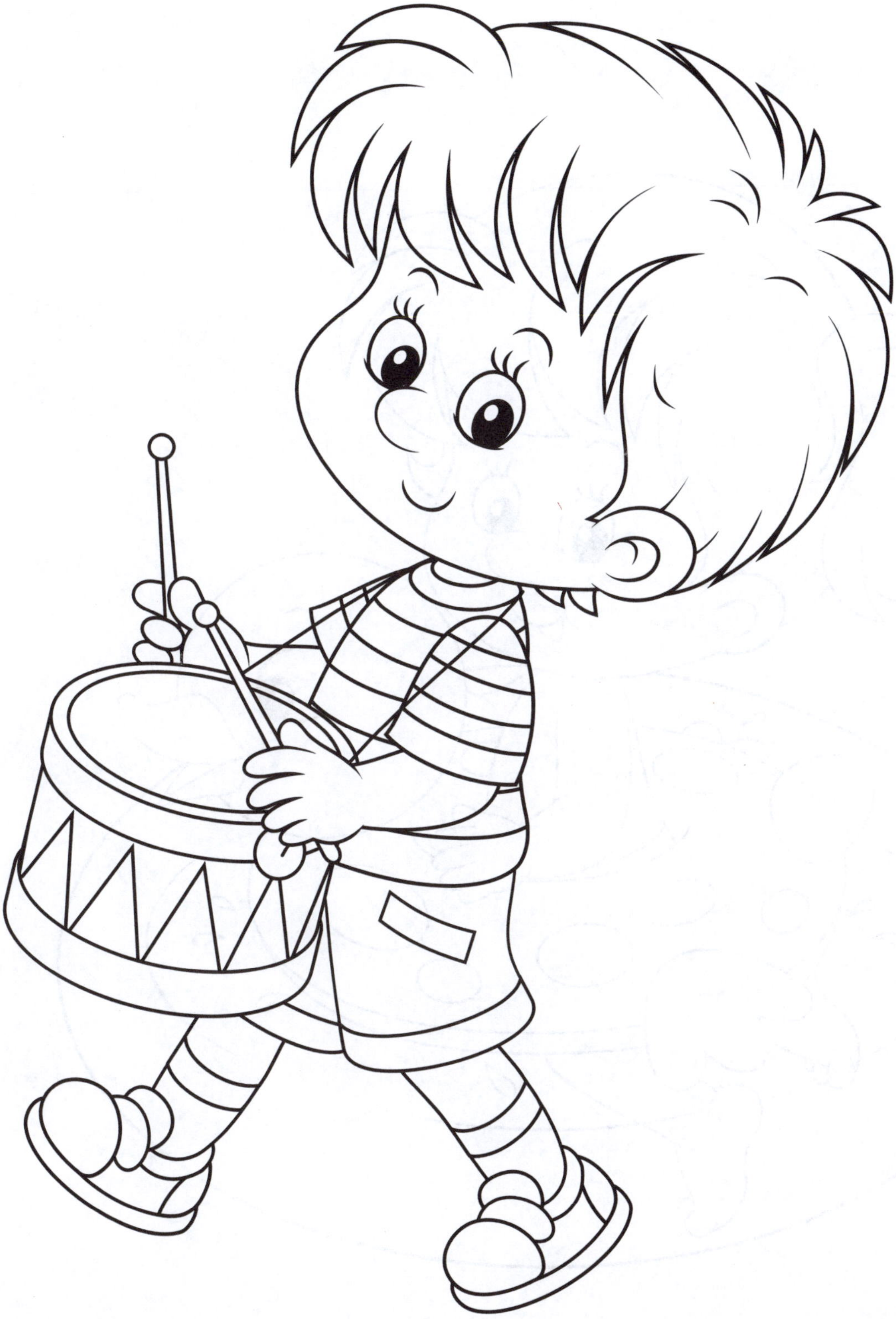

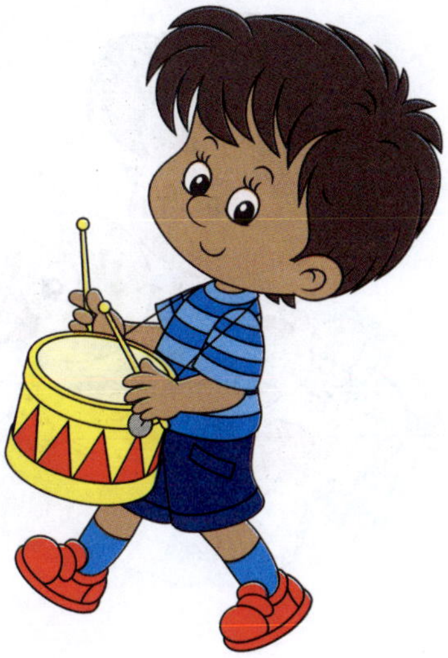

drum

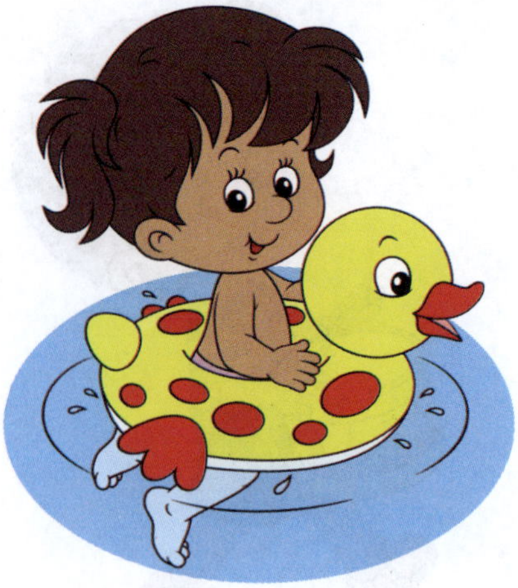

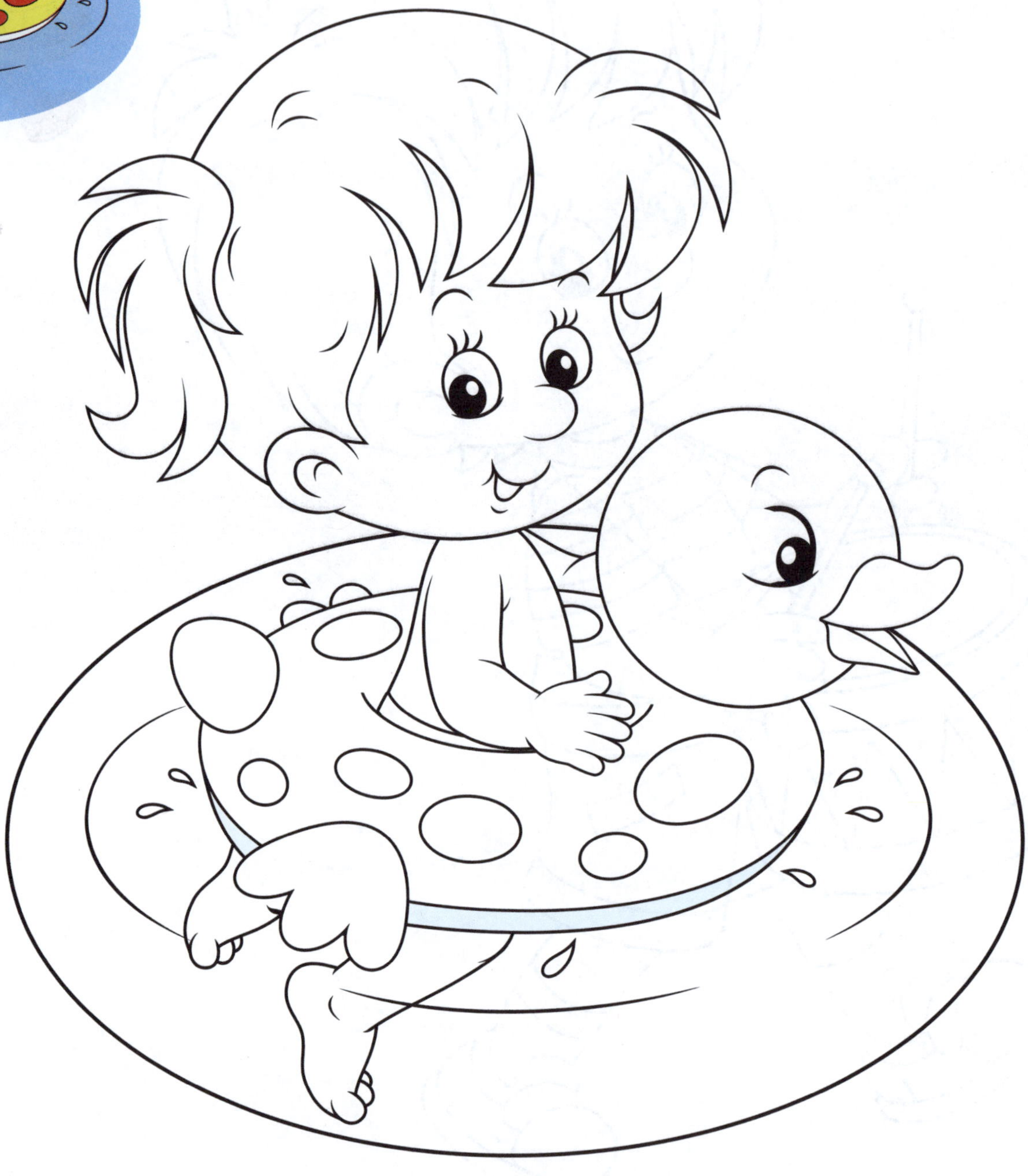

paddling pool

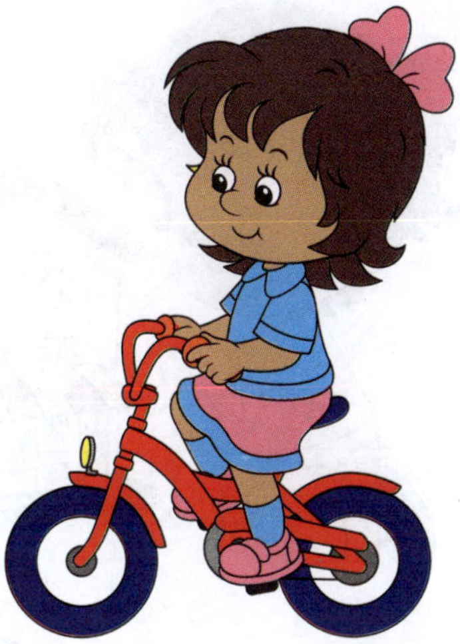

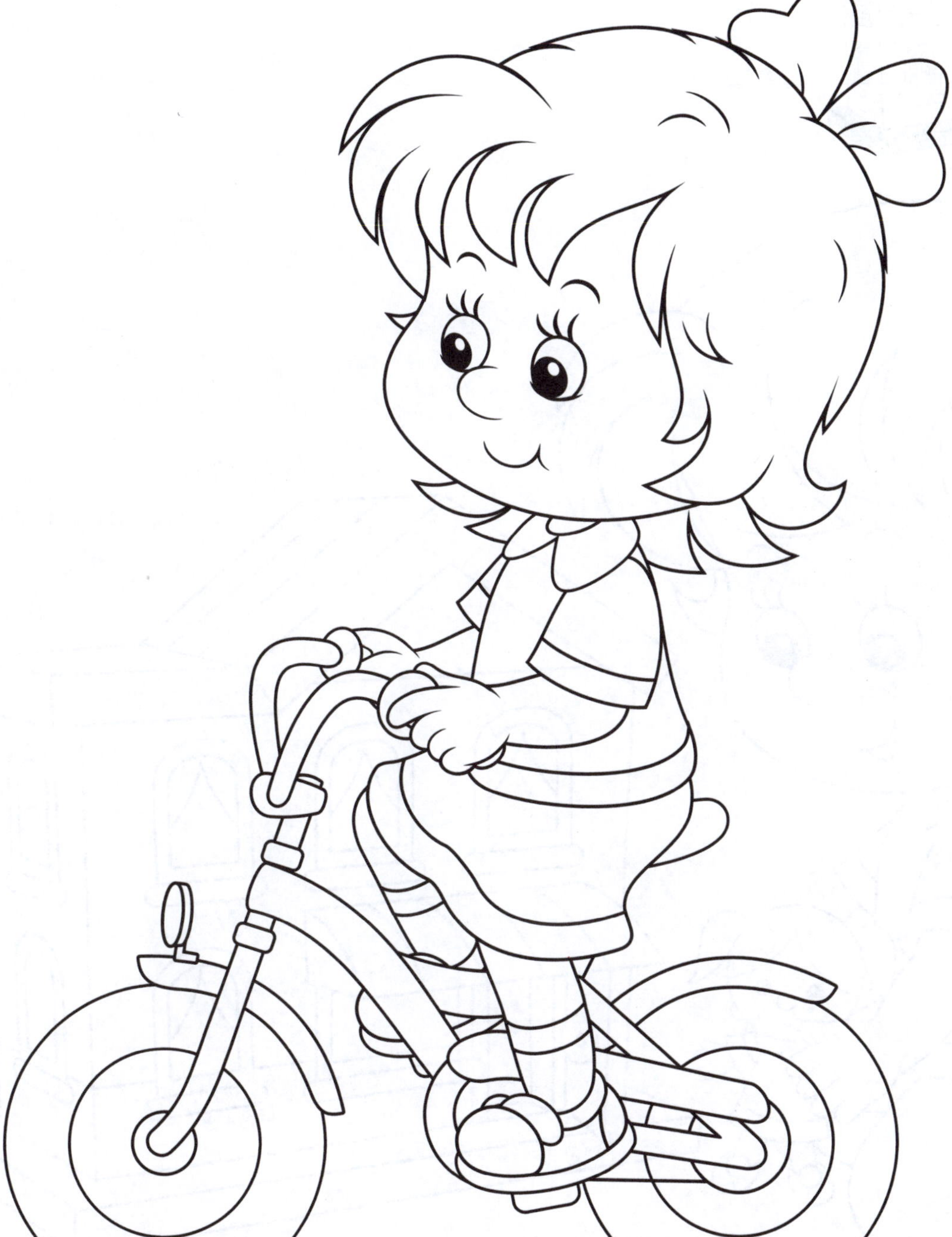

cycling

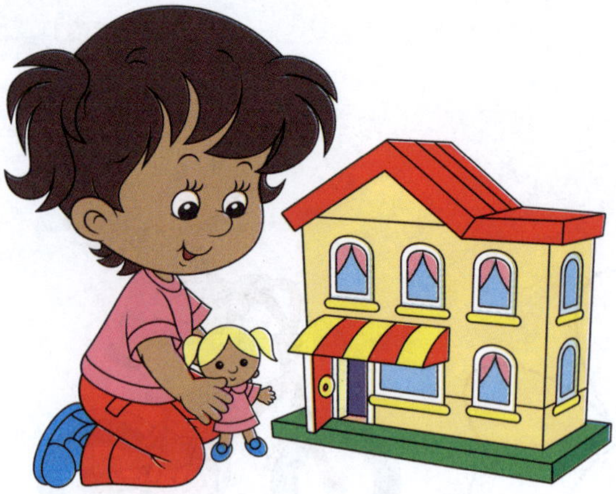

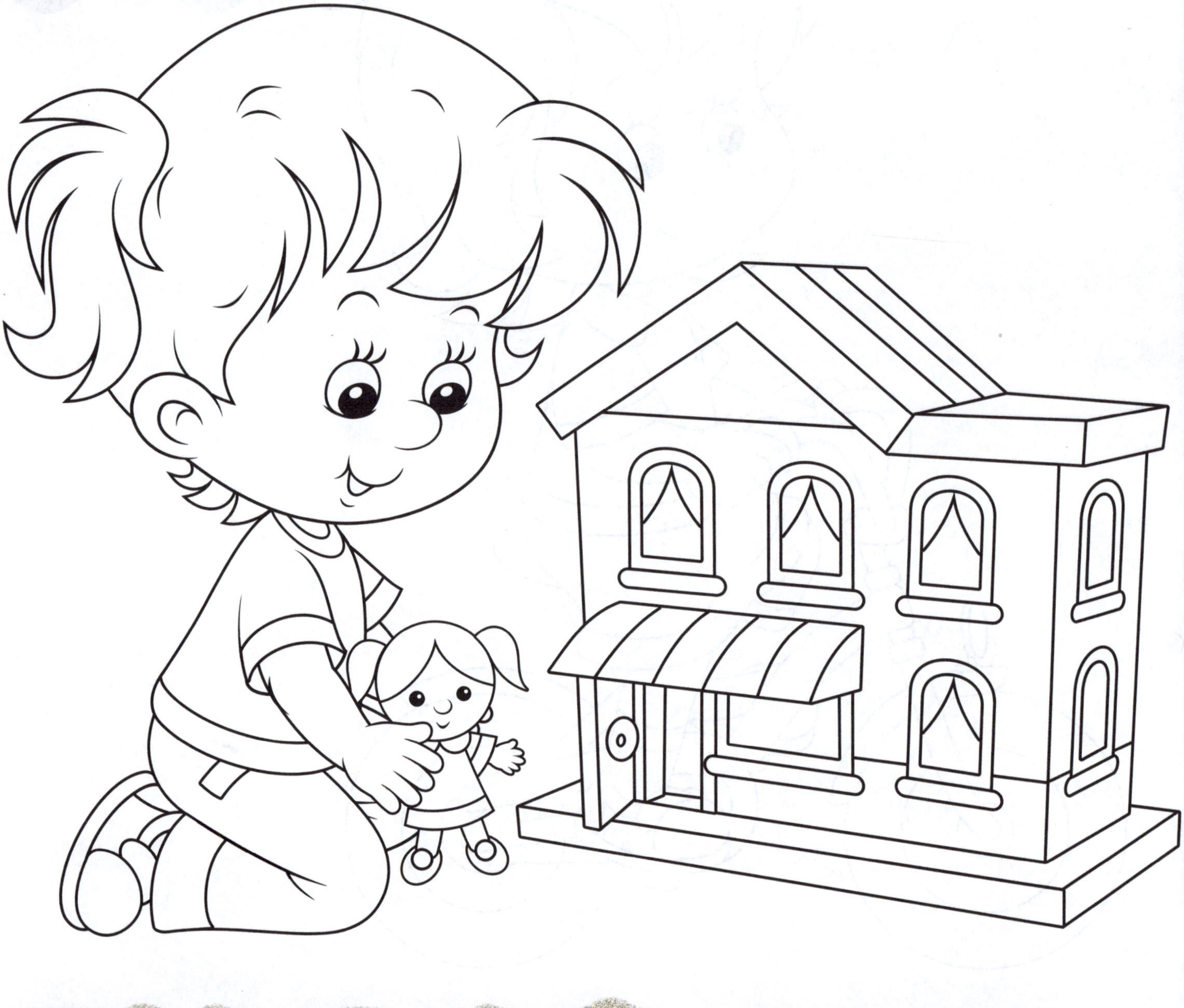

doll's house